THE GARDENER'S
LITTLE INSTRUCTION
BOOK

Also available from Thorsons

A BABY'S LITTLE INSTRUCTION BOOK
David Brawn
A CAT'S LITTLE INSTRUCTION BOOK
Leigh W. Rutledge
A DOG'S LITTLE INSTRUCTION BOOK
David Brawn
THE DRIVER'S LITTLE INSTRUCTION BOOK
Mike Leonard
THE FISHERMAN'S LITTLE INSTRUCTION BOOK
Rod Rest
LIFE'S LITTLE INSTRUCTION BOOK
H. Jackson Brown Jr
LIFE'S LITTLE INSTRUCTION BOOK VOLUME II
H. Jackson Brown Jr
THE LOVERS' LITTLE INSTRUCTION BOOK
Cindy Francis
THE OFFICE LIFE LITTLE INSTRUCTION BOOK
Holly Budd
THE PARENT'S LITTLE INSTRUCTION BOOK
Cindy Francis
THE SALESMAN'S LITTLE INSTRUCTION BOOK
Sean McArthur
THE SCOT'S LITTLE INSTRUCTION BOOK
Tony Sweeney
A TEDDY BEAR'S LITTLE INSTRUCTION BOOK
David and Tracey Brawn

THE GARDENER'S LITTLE INSTRUCTION BOOK

Violet Wood

Thorsons
An Imprint of HarperCollinsPublishers

Thorsons
An Imprint of HarperCollins*Publishers*
77–85 Fulham Palace Road
Hammersmith, London W6 8JB

Published by Thorsons 1996
1 3 5 7 9 10 8 6 4 2

© Violet Wood 1996

Violet Wood asserts the moral right to
be identified as the author of this work

A catalogue record for this book is available from the British Library

ISBN 0 7225 3286 5

Text illustrations by Mike Gordon

Printed in Great Britain by HarperCollinsManufacturing Glasgow

In memory of my grandmother
who first inspired me to garden

Introduction

Gardening is probably one of the most popular leisure pursuits there is. For some it's a passion, even perhaps an obsession; for others it's a pleasant way to idle away a sunny afternoon.

For me gardening is therapy. I am rarely more at peace than when working in my garden. Life seems to be problem-free when you're concentrating on weeding, digging or planting. And, oh, the joy of gathering armfuls of flowers or vegetables.

I first became interested in gardening as a small child when I stayed with my grandparents deep in the heart of the Garden of England – Kent. My grandmother never read gardening books, but she seemed to be a fount of knowledge and her garden was a mass of blooms, fruits and vegetables. Some of her tips I've passed on here, others I've gathered over the years from fellow gardeners. I've also thrown in a sprinkling of gardening thoughts to amuse and inspire you.

If you, like me, enjoy gardening, then I hope you will enjoy this little book.

Everyone needs a garden of their own

 Look at weeding as one of life's therapies

 Don't throw snails over your garden wall

 It's fine to dream, but work at making
your dream garden a reality

Sow and transplant only with a waxing, never a waning, moon

 Get your lawn-mower overhauled *before* the grass-cutting season begins

 Order your seeds in the winter, from the comfort of your armchair

Make sure you have some Japanese anemones – they are a wonderful standby, blooming from late summer through to autumn, and the white version makes a splendid background plant for bright colours

Don't procrastinate, rather get ahead

Nothing looks nicer than a collection of nicely weathered terracotta pots

 Keep your shed tidy – that way you'll be able to find what you need

 Aquilegias are perfect perennials for a low maintenance garden, with both glorious flowers and attractive foliage

Don't be disappointed if all your seeds don't germinate

 Listen to your plants, as well as talking to them

 Avoid falling in the pond

 Be patient

Plant heliotrope for its sensational cherry-pie perfume

 For reliable autumn colour, plant the deciduous varieties of cotoneaster and berberis

 Don't worry about mistakes – that's how you learn

Nasturtiums make a bright showing of red, yellow and orange, but like a poor soil, so do not feed them

Be sure to keep a patch of nettles
– butterflies love them

 Plant marigolds next to your carrots
– root fly hate the smell

 Do gardening jobs as soon as you see
they need doing

Keep a garden notebook, because you won't remember where everything is planted, or when you planted it

 Sow some hardy annuals to edge a border

 Always carry secateurs – you're bound to need them

Learn botanical names

 Remember that a bright sunny morning may be just that, so don't put off tasks that have to be done and find it's raining

 Keep greenfly off your roses by underplanting with clumps of chives

Take a nap occasionally

 Plant hollyhocks, sunflowers, mulleins, foxgloves, delphiniums and giant dahlias at the back of borders

 Check you have everything you need before you set off to the bottom of the garden

Plant a buddleia and watch the butterflies dance

 Be satisfied with your accomplishments

 Do some gentle backward stretching to compensate for too much bending

Wallflowers are not merely for window-boxes – they look excellent planted irregularly in gaps in borders and can be pulled out after flowering

The watching and the waiting teach important lessons for life

Always grow a few pots of good summer
annuals such as nicotianas – they
make wonderful space-fillers
when other plants have
died down

If you have a shady border, the best plants are monkshood, Japanese anemone, astrantia, astilbe, bergenia, brunnera, hosta, lamium, aquilegia and Solomon's seal

 Be generous with your cuttings

 Wear a hat when it's hot

Look out for Gertrude Jekyll's books – she was one of the twentieth century's most influential gardeners

 Take time to wonder

 Listen to the weather forecast – frosts can strike unexpectedly

Plant penstemons to freshen up parched borders – they are ideal late summer perennials

 Understand when to prune and when not to prune

 Tend your compost heap with love

To brighten up a dull patch of garden border, sprinkle poppy seeds over it in the spring

 The experience of growing things is healing

Nothing shakes off depression quicker than a little time spent working in the garden

 Don't be lazy about staking your plants

 Even in the depths of winter, there are signs of life to come

Always put your gardening shoes on, even if you think you'll keep to the pathways – you never do

 Save your empty loo rolls – they make great planters for starting off sweet peas

 Save your empty plastic bottles – cut in half they make superb individual cloches

Water your seedlings with care and watch them grow

 Planting a garden brings untold happiness

 Don't grumble about the autumn clear-up – debris and bonfires are part of the process and have their own charm

Birds are wonderful companions when you're digging

 Every day is the opportunity to create something beautiful

 Take care of your soil

Lilies make delightful pot plants for the house or conservatory, but do keep the compost moist and feed them with a little bonemeal in the spring

 Liquid seaweed is a marvellous tonic for your plants

Learn to love rain – it is as necessary as the sun

 Remember the saying 'Sow one seed for the rook, one for the crow, one to die and one to grow'

 Find out from neighbouring gardeners what grows well locally

Don't disturb the worms

 Save your autumn leaves – once rotted down (separate from your compost) they make a superb mulch for spring weeds

 Don't sow seed when the ground is too cold

Don't overdo it

 Rotate your vegetables to prevent the soil from becoming exhausted

 Don't wash your face in the bird bath

 Water gardens should not look like a lawn of duckweed

Remember that Nature is never idle, even if you are

 Avoid gnomes

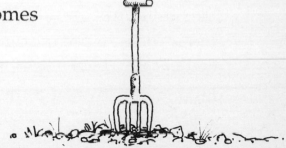

Never plant Leyland cypress if you want to be taken seriously

 The best hardy annuals for summer colour include pot marigold, candytuft, clarkia, cornflower, godetia, larkspur, mignonette, love-in-a-mist, poppies and sweet peas

Don't ruin your garden with badly chosen furniture

 Do not plant a tree too near to the house

 Grow some borage with your strawberries – they make excellent companions

The common foxglove stimulates growth of neighbouring plants and helps disease resistance

 Sow turnip seed thickly if you want to get rid of couch grass

 You can always try *eating* ground elder – use the young leaves as for spinach

Grow Mexican marigolds (*Tagetes signata pumila*) to control ground elder or horsetail

Don't worry about your plants spilling over lawn edges – tidiness is not a virtue

 Leave your classy labels dangling so everyone can see you've been to the right nursery

 Mix old-fashioned shrub roses with repeat-flowering ones

Don't always follow the advice of old herbals, particularly those which suggest naked seed-sowing

Join the Royal Horticultural Society

If you really want to impress, join the Soil Association and the Henry Doubleday Research Association

Tea leaves are an excellent mulch for camellias and roses

 Avoid Pampas grass

 Grow herbs everywhere – not only will you have a constant supply for cooking, but they also help keep pests away from your fruit and vegetables

Dahlias seem to prefer their own bed or corner rather than being mixed in with other flowers

Weedkiller is only permissible on paths and drives

 Avoid crazy paving – york stone is better

 Climbing plants are essential to cover brick or stonework

Don't forget the edible flowers – pot marigolds, nasturtiums, violets, borage

 If you want to gather roses, mind the thorns

 Avoid gimmicky gadgets – they're not necessary

Make dandelion wine (that's one way of getting rid of them) but don't drink too much of it

 Never go on holiday in summer – you might miss something

 Water tubs and containers daily in hot weather

Don't trust anyone else in the garden
– they're bound to think your prize plants
are weeds and pull them up

Remember that the young think gardening is the passion of the middle-aged because they have grown too old for sex

 Keep off the garden in frost and snow

 Never give up

There is always the right place for the right plant

 It's no good lying in bed thinking of everything to be done

 Your garden is a reflection of your state of mind

A mulch is a weeder's best friend

 Good soil, like good looks, isn't something you're born with

 Grow giant vegetables just for fun

 You can't necessarily trust the experts, but you can your instincts

Frost and snow will rid you of some of the garden's enemies

 The secret of abundance is careful husbandry

 Make your flower beds large and your borders wide

Before you light a bonfire, check there isn't a hedgehog hibernating in it

 Don't envy others their gardens – think of all the work that goes into them

 Lean on your hoe from time to time

Every gardener knows something you don't, so learn from others

 Accept help – you cannot do it alone

 Remember, one year's weeds, seven years' seeds

Other people's tools work only in other people's gardens

 Even a window-box reveals something about its owner

 Watch your feet when using a scythe

Do not line your garden pond with turquoise PVC – it is not a public swimming bath

When putting in new plants, don't press down too heavily – use finger pressure

If a plant looks dead, give it the benefit of the doubt for a few more weeks – it will probably start to perk up

 Don't say there isn't time – you can always find time if you want to

 You need a little optimism

Break the rules and let vegetables go
to seed occasionally – flowers and
seedheads can be stunning

 Don't be afraid to move a plant to a
different position

 Use urns and jardinières to make a focal
point in your garden

Plant annuals like poached egg plant (*Limnanthes douglasii*) between your herbs and vegetables

 Keep plants clear of aphids by companion planting or use pirimicarb, which will not harm other more beneficial insects

 Watch your fingers when using loppers

Remember what that famous gardener Gertrude Jekyll said – 'A garden is far more than just a collection of plants'

 Don't stand underneath your hanging baskets when watering them

 Summer savory will keep onion fly from your onions

Visit the Royal National Rose Society Garden in Hertfordshire – it is one of the best places to see roses

 Pray for rain

 While most herbs grow easily, parsley is notoriously difficult to get started

Trim your lawn edges to set off both lawn and borders

 Grow mint, sage, thyme or rosemary alongside your cabbages

 Face facts – the only way to stop cats digging in your borders is not to have any borders

Don't let your garden turn you into a snob – four apple trees do not an orchard make

 If you cannot arrange for someone to water your container plants whilst you are away on holiday, move them into the shade after a good soaking

Find out whether plants prefer sun or shade

 Shroud your carrots, celery and cabbages in finely spun fleece to protect against root flies

Employ a gardener – but take the credit for his handiwork

 When dead-heading roses, also remove the suckers at the base

 If you need some rain, light the barbecue

Gardening is about sharing the problems as well as the remedies

 Do not have turf laid during a hosepipe ban

 If you want to avoid pesticides, use derris or insecticidal soap

Grow low-growing annuals like
ageratums, busy lizzies and gazanias
on sunny window-sills

 Be *very* sure before you eat any
mushrooms from your garden

 Colour-theme your containers rather than
having a mass of different colours

Grow vegetables such as ruby chard and red cabbage in the flower border for visual as well as edible benefit

Embrace diversity – a wide range of crops and varieties will help combat pests and diseases

 Borage leaves are essential for Pimms

 Listen to Gardeners' Question Time

Walk around the garden early in the morning and at twilight to spot any problems – undesirable pests are more likely to be lurking then

 Nasturtiums are a good companion for apples

Buy a copy of *Gardens of England and Wales* each year – it lists over 3,000 private gardens to visit

 Use a small onion hoe to weed densely planted beds

Remember that it's snobs who tell you that you should only grow old-fashioned roses

 Always water plants in the evening during hot weather

 Plant a scented shrub by your door to greet visitors

Try a coir dust based compost instead of peat

 Don't expect your sundial to take account of Summer Time

 Plant your garden to look like Vita Sackville-West's

Think in terms of feeding the soil, rather than feeding the plant

 Hostas are excellent as marginal plants beside a pond or stream

 Make sure that you garden with love

If you need a little inspiration, buy a gardening magazine or send off for some catalogues

 Take cuttings of tender plants like penstemons or hebes as an insurance against losses in a bad winter

Make sure your sprinkler is facing the right way when you turn it on

 Choose plants with pretty foliage as well as flowers, like hepaticas

 Remember that many common garden plants are poisonous, e.g. rhododendrons, laburnum, yew

Buy the very best tools you can afford, stainless steel if possible

 Use annuals to fill in any gaps in herbaceous borders

 Site your garden pool where there is plenty of sunshine

Never put off picking courgettes until tomorrow

 Don't devote your life to cultivating a garden and then hang a permanent washing line across the middle of it

 Tend your garden and you will find peace of mind

Remember that life began in a garden

 Keep a gardening diary to compare what you did in previous years

 Wipe your tools with an oily cloth after use for maximum life

Remember that you get second chances
with gardening – there's always the next
season

 Plant shows are an excellent opportunity
to pick up useful tips from the growers

 Rotted down newspaper, finely shredded,
can help suppress weeds

Choose perennials which produce attractive foliage and will make an impact in their first season, e.g. *Alchemilla vulgaris* (lady's mantle), which is easy to grow and the perfect foil for brightly coloured plants

 If your garden is immaculate, get a sign saying 'Beware of the Gardener'

Use a barrier of ash or sharp grit to deter slugs from eating perennials

 Send away for seed catalogues each year – they are full of ideas and gardening advice

 Always clean pots and seed trays carefully with garden disinfectant

Jerusalem artichokes make an excellent windbreak in the vegetable garden

 Be sure to earth up potatoes to prevent tubers from becoming green and poisonous

Plant monkshood (*Aconitum napellus*) at the back of the flower border – all bugs, slugs and caterpillars will avoid it because of its extremely poisonous nature

 Do not place tender plants in an east-facing situation – the early morning sun in winter will cause damage

Always deadhead roses with secateurs
and cut back to a leaf or bud

 Leave filled watering cans to warm up in
the greenhouse so that seedlings don't
have the shock of cold water

 Plant runner and french beans in the most
sheltered part of the vegetable garden

Feed roses with a slow-release fertilizer like bonemeal in the spring

 In dry weather remember that a good soak for plants and containers is better than a drizzle every day

 Discuss your garden with friends and neighbours and exchange cuttings

Do not get a dog if you value your lawn

 Don't light a bonfire too close to the trees

 Trim the roots and leaves of leeks before planting in an oversized hole, then fill the hole with water

Remember that work done in the spring will cut out twice as much in the summer

 Plant a clove of garlic by each rose to ward off vampires – and greenfly

 Remember that weeds are opportunists

Never despair if your garden is bordered by overhanging trees – plant hawthorne and hazel, dog roses, honeysuckle and clematis

 The art of good mulching is to block out weeds, encourage the roots of plants and retain moisture

Do not plant merely for dreamy summers

 Always sow seeds thinly – crowded
seedlings never grow well

 Mix dust-like seeds with a pinch of dry
silver sand to make sowing easier

Grow red and green salad bowl lettuce at the front of the flower border

 It does not do to rush things in the garden – a shrub may take 10 years to flower, a tree 100 years to reach maturity

 Water pots and trays from below after sowing

Don't be fooled into thinking it's all as quick and easy as on *Gardener's World*

 In a drought, use your bath water on the garden – but fish the soap out first

 Read, look, think and plan

 Know your weeds

Most shrubs should be pruned immediately after flowering

 Cover fruit bushes with netting to keep the birds away

 Remember to turn seed-trays on window-sills round each day

Hoe on dry days

 Don't scorn the onion family – it is a source of spectacular beauty and terrific for companion planting

 Try growing sweetcorn at the back of the flower border

Watch for gifts of new plants

 When tidying the garden for winter,
don't cut everything down.
A layer of dead growth
protects from frosts

Do not waste water. Instead:

i) incorporate organic matter into the soil to act as a sponge

ii) grow plants close together so that the leaves join in a protective umbrella

iii) apply a mulch to stop evaporation

Do not leave the soil bare over the winter – apply a mulch or grow a green manure like grazing rye or winter tares

 Seek out old varieties of vegetables – they are less dependent on chemical input and will also have better flavour

 Armchair gardening is OK too

Save yourself some backache – don't double-dig and leave the soil micro-organisms in peace

 Though it's nice to cut some flowers for inside, leave some in the garden

 Keep a log of interesting birds or animals that visit your garden

Always plant fresh bulbs in containers, transferring old ones, once the foliage has died down, to the garden

 Wear gloves at all times if you want your hands to look attractive

 Keep off the soil in winter or you will compact it

In the vegetable garden, cover some areas with polythene or plastic cloches to warm the soil prior to planting

 When sowing, remember that little and often is best – that way you can keep a succession of plants going

Prune so that it looks as if you haven't touched the plant

 Don't mow your lawn too short – a little growth protects the roots during drought and hot sun

 There is nothing nicer than propagating a few plants to give as presents

Make your garden a haven for wildlife and let nature solve the problem of pests

 Don't leave things to chance – plant supports should be put in the border before the plants have grown too tall

 If soil sticks to your boots in spring, wait until it is drier before forking over

Remember that rain can damage your soil by leaching out nutrients

 Remember the Chinese proverb 'He who plants a garden, plants happiness'

 Low-growing hedges such as box or lavender make a charming edge for flower or vegetable beds

Gardening is an exercise in letting go

 Learn to live in the garden if you want to live off it

 Don't be put off by the smell of blood, bone and fishmeal – they are organic and do your plants a power of good

Plant pennyroyal to ward off ants

 Be in touch with what the garden wants by 'listening' to it

 Don't be fooled – April and May can be treacherous months

Encourage thrushes, moles and frogs
– they will keep the slug and snail
population down

 If the lush green leaves on your camellias
turn yellow, give them a tonic of iron
sequestrene

If plain green shoots start appearing on your variegated plants, cut them off at the base

 Remember the summer-flowering bulbs – lilies, gladiolii and alliums

 Raze your chives to the ground and you will get another crop

Don't scoff at hardy annuals – they are a cheap and cheerful means of providing colour

 Don't be afraid to experiment with pips – lemon, orange and grapefruit pips can all grow into handsome trees

When visiting the Chelsea Flower Show, wear comfortable shoes, don't drink too much Pimms and although it's OK to sniff, don't on any account take cuttings

 Don't get too carried away at Chelsea and order plants inappropriate for your garden

But do buy some seeds at Chelsea

Dead-head seedpods of daffodils to give stronger bulbs

 Remember that pot plants on window-sills need a lighter mixture of soil

 French marigolds attract useful insects, while the smell repels those you don't want

In order to work your garden, get
to know the soil, the aspect and the
micro-climate

 It always helps to know what other
gardeners have done

 Plant up hanging baskets but leave inside
until they look mature and colourful

Pests, diseases and weeds have no scruples – they appear in the best of gardens

 Leave the digging and aerating to the worms – they pull down the goodness from your mulch into the topsoil

 Become fond of the hoe

If the ground is badly infested with perennial weeds, smother them and deprive them of light

 Another use for old tights – cut them into strips to make soft, strong ties for below flower spikes

Remember that your garden reveals a lot of clues about your personality

 Regular dead-heading encourages more flowers

 Encourage hoverflies to act as nature's pest controllers by planting *Convolvulus tricolor* and other flowers

Always check sowing instructions on seed packets

If you have trouble with slugs and snails, good flowers to plant are bleeding heart (*Dicentra spectabilis*), sedum, aquilegia and forget-me-nots (*Myosotis*) – they seem to resist them

Always harden off young plants raised in a greenhouse before planting out

 Don't be afraid about not being overly clean and tidy – hedgehogs, beetles and spiders love a pile of rubbish and will help fight pests

When digging, don't automatically reach for the spade – a fork does a better job and is kinder to worms

 When visiting a garden centre, never buy a plant which is dry at the roots

 Catalogues are crucial for the long winter nights

Remember that most parts of plants can be used for propagation – a stem, root or leaf cutting, a sucker or division – as well as seeds

 When planting out in dry conditions, always water the hole before you put the plant in, mulch with organic matter and then water thoroughly

You will always feel better in the garden

 Choose trees that are even more fascinating in winter than in summer, like *Sorbus hupehensis*, which has ferny green leaves, autumn colour and pink-tinged white berries

Remember that a garden should never be a riot of colour – rather follow the Gertrude Jekyll principle of brightly coloured plants in the centre and more pastel shades towards the edges of a border

 There are always ideas to copy or adapt, so visit as many gardens as possible

Collecting plants is like collecting anything – make sure that you keep it under control

 Remember the saying about ivy – 'The first year it sleeps, the second year it creeps, the third year it leaps'

Once your perennials have finished flowering, give them a good watering then decapitate them – they will push forth bright new growth within a very short time

 Day lilies (*Hemerocallis*) will settle anywhere and last for years, and are one of the best herbaceous perennials

Split your herbaceous plants every three years or so

 Good summer flowers for containers in a hot dry spot, or on a roof garden, are osteospermums, mesembryanthemums and Californian poppies (*Eschscholtzia californica*)

Grow mignonette for its beautiful
perfume

 Scatter grit around your alpine plants
– it enhances their appearance and also
ensures that they are not damaged by rain
splashing soil on to them

 A garden is never finished

For a beautiful display in spring, plant less familiar bulbs like snake's head fritillaries (*Fritillaria meleagris*)

 For winter flowers and fragrance, plant Chinese viburnums, particularly *Viburnum farreri* or the large flowered *Viburnum bodnantense*

A beautiful garden is like a beautiful painting – it does not reveal itself all at once

 Vegetables can be ornamental as well as tasty

For winter colour, plant viburnum
(*Viburnum fragrans*), winter jasmine,
flowering quince, hollies, ivies,
periwinkle, heathers and daphne
(*Daphne mezereum*)

Don't get depressed when you return
from a holiday to find your garden has
become unruly

Miracles happen

 Share your produce

 Truly, you reap what you sow